Bubble Homes and Fish Farts

Fiona Bayrock

Illustrated by
Carolyn Conahan

iii Charlesbridge

For my mom, to whom I owe countless bottles of dish soap
and many summer days filled with bubble-chasing laughter.
With love—F. B.

To my mom, Katharine R. Digby, and Pat Robertson, and
great science teachers everywhere, for passing along their
interest in all things interesting, which is everything,
more or less—C. C.

Text copyright © 2009 by Fiona Bayrock
Illustrations copyright © 2009 by Carolyn Conahan
All rights reserved, including the right of reproduction in whole or in part in any form.
Charlesbridge and colophon are registered trademarks of Charlesbridge Publishing, Inc.

Published by Charlesbridge
85 Main Street
Watertown, MA 02472
(617) 926-0329
www.charlesbridge.com

Library of Congress Cataloging-in-Publication Data
Bayrock, Fiona.
    Bubble homes and fish farts / Fiona Bayrock; illustrated by
Carolyn Conahan.
       p. cm.
    ISBN 978-1-57091-669-4 (reinforced for library use)
    ISBN 978-1-57091-670-0 (softcover)
1. Animals—Juvenile literature. 2. Bubbles—Juvenile literature.
I. Conahan, Carolyn, ill. II. Title.
QL49.B39 2009
590—dc22

Printed in China
(hc) 10 9 8 7 6 5 4 3 2 1
(sc) 10 9 8 7 6 5 4 3 2 1

Illustrations done in watercolor on 140-lb. extra-white hot-press Fabriano Artistico paper
Display type set in Flora Dora, designed by Nick Curtis
Text type set in Goudy, designed by Frederic W. Goudy
Color separations by Chroma Graphics, Singapore
Printed and bound by Regent Publishing Services
Production supervision by Brian G. Walker
Designed by Susan Mallory Sherman

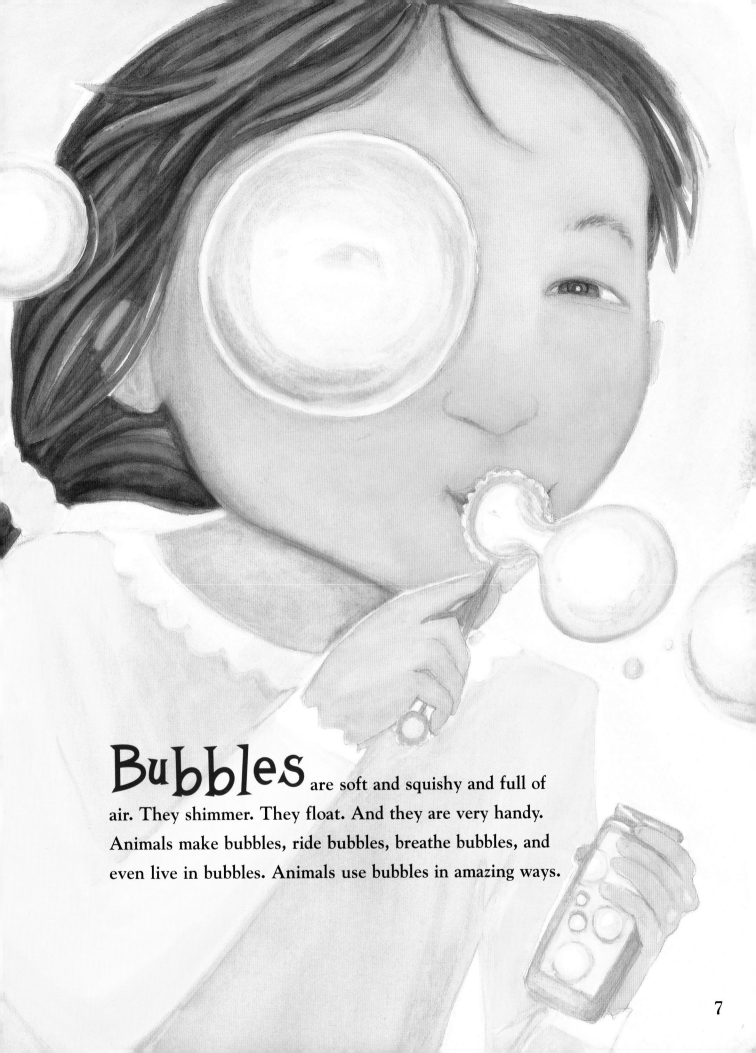

Bubbles are soft and squishy and full of air. They shimmer. They float. And they are very handy. Animals make bubbles, ride bubbles, breathe bubbles, and even live in bubbles. Animals use bubbles in amazing ways.

BUBBLES ARE FOR SAILING.

Violet Sea Snail • *Janthina janthina*

Violet sea snails can't swim. Instead, they sail along the ocean surface on rafts made of bubbles. First, a snail oozes a blob of bubbles that hardens. Then the snail hangs upside down from its floating bubble raft. It drifts with the wind and the currents, feeding on small surface animals it happens to find. The bubble raft doesn't break, because the snails are lightweight, thanks to their paper-thin shells and small size—about the size of a large grape. Very few shelled animals live at the surface. This means violet sea snails can feast on food that most shelled ocean animals can't reach.

9

BUBBLES ARE FOR RUNNING.

Water Shrew • *Sorex palustris*

With a name like "water shrew," it's no surprise that this tiny mammal is an expert swimmer. Over and over, it dives to the bottoms of mountain lakes and streams, searching for insect nymphs and small fish to eat. Many water-loving animals have webbed feet to help them swim. The water shrew has hind feet that work like swim fins, but they aren't webbed. Instead, they have a fringe of rigid hairs around each toe that does the job. The hairs also trap air bubbles under the feet—enough that the shrew can actually run on top of the water for several seconds at a time.

No, it's not
a miracle.
But it is a very
good trick!

BUBBLES ARE FOR BREATHING.

Backswimmer • *Notonecta glauca*

Like scuba divers, backswimmer bugs take two containers of air underwater with them so they can breathe. The backswimmer's air containers are pockets on its body. Clinging upside down to an underwater plant, the backswimmer looks up for mosquito larvae, small tadpoles, and other unsuspecting prey. When something tasty comes along, the backswimmer's bubbles carry it up for the attack. It can also chase prey by paddling long, powerful hind legs like boat oars. Backswimmers can stay underwater for hours before riding their bubbles to the surface for fresh air.

BUBBLES ARE FOR KEEPING WARM.

Sea Otter • *Enhydra lutris*

Sea otters spend their lives in cold ocean water—swimming, floating, diving for food, eating, having babies, and even sleeping. Most sea mammals have a thick layer of fat under the skin to protect them from the cold. Otters don't. So how do they stay warm? Bubbles to the rescue! Sea otters blow bubbles and whisk the water to make even more bubbles. Then they rub the bubbles into their fur. Sea otter hairs are shaped to "zip lock" together to keep air bubbles in and cold water out. The layer of air trapped in the dense underhair works like a down comforter to help sea otters stay warm.

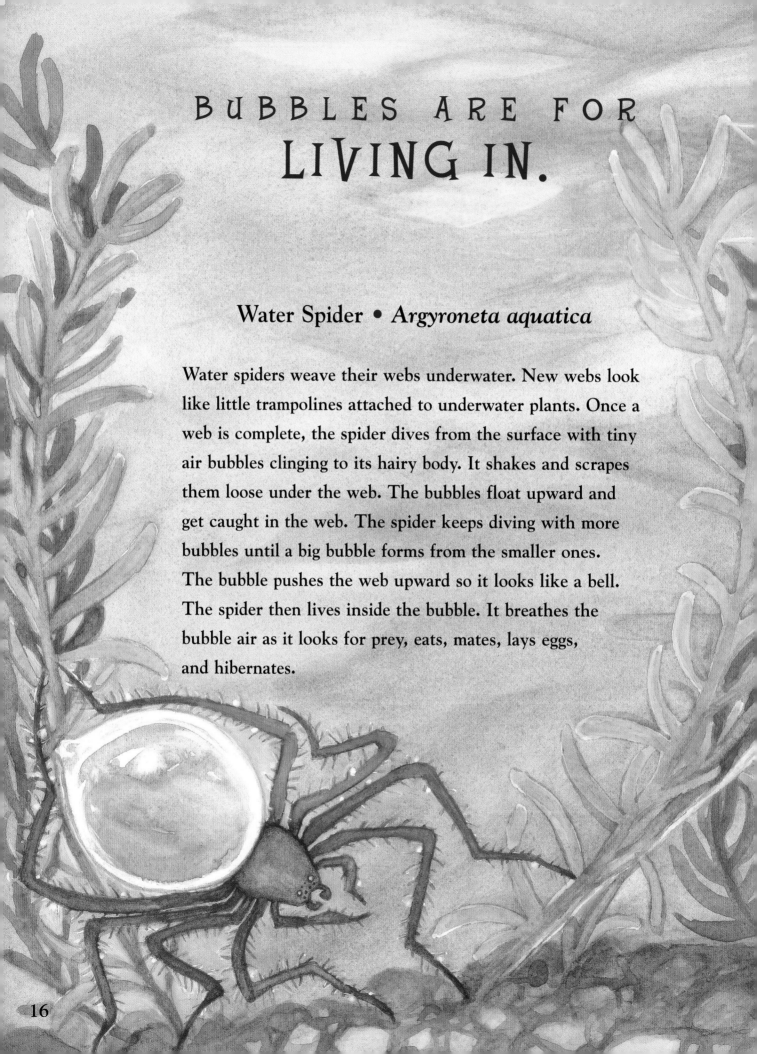

BUBBLES ARE FOR LIVING IN.

Water Spider • *Argyroneta aquatica*

Water spiders weave their webs underwater. New webs look like little trampolines attached to underwater plants. Once a web is complete, the spider dives from the surface with tiny air bubbles clinging to its hairy body. It shakes and scrapes them loose under the web. The bubbles float upward and get caught in the web. The spider keeps diving with more bubbles until a big bubble forms from the smaller ones. The bubble pushes the web upward so it looks like a bell. The spider then lives inside the bubble. It breathes the bubble air as it looks for prey, eats, mates, lays eggs, and hibernates.

Cozy.

BUBBLES ARE FOR FINDING FOOD.

Star-nosed Mole • *Condylura cristata*

The star-nosed mole feels and smells its way underground and underwater. The fleshy star nose works like a bunch of super fingers, touching, touching, here, there, and everywhere, searching for something good to eat. Star-nosed moles also have a good sense of smell, even when underwater. As it swims, a mole blows bubbles from its nose and breathes them back in. A quick sniff of the bubble air tells the mole if lunch is nearby and which way to go to find it. Fish and worms—yummy meals for a star-nosed mole— leave underwater scent trails. These scents in the water mix with the bubble air. Swimming moles sniff to follow scent trails underwater just as dogs do on land.

Not me!

Not me!

19

BUBBLES ARE FOR FISHING.

Humpback Whale • *Megaptera novaeangliae*

With a mouth the size of a small living room, the humpback whale opens wide and swims through a school of herring. Powerful muscles push the mega-mouthful of water out again through baleen plates. The baleen is made of fingernail material, so it's strong and flexible. It works like a sieve to trap the fish, which are then swallowed whole. Humpbacks work together to get the most fish per scoop. One whale releases streams of bubbles while swimming in a circle. This makes a bubble net that herds fish into a tight group. Then several whales—maybe a dozen or more—swim up through the bubble net with mouths open wide. What teamwork!

They fall
for it
every time!
Silly fish.

21

BUBBLES ARE FOR CHASING PREY.

Weddell Seal • *Leptonychotes weddellii*

Weddell seals swim far and dive deep under the Antarctic sea ice to catch hundreds of fish each day. This seal can be sneaky, sometimes swimming within a few inches of a fish before the fish notices. Fish hide from seals in the bumpy underside of the ice. Looking up, seals see the dark fish shapes against the sunlight shining through the ice. But the fish are tucked in the cracks and out of reach. When this happens, the Weddell seal blows a stream of bubbles. The bubbles chase the fish out of hiding, the seal charges forward, and—gulp!—lunch.

BUBBLES ARE FOR TALKING.

Herring
Clupea pallasii (Pacific)
Clupea harengus (Atlantic)

Each night thousands of herring gather near the ocean surface and release streams of bubbles from their backsides. That's right: fish farts. Well, sort of. To be true "flatulence" —that's the scientific word for "fart"—the gas should come from digesting food. But the herring farts, or Fast Repetitive Ticks (FaRTs) as the scientists call them, come from air the herring have gulped at the surface, not from food the fish have eaten. Scientists think FaRTing might be a way that herring "talk" when it's too dark to see each other. Most other fish can't hear the herring FaRTs, so herring can signal each other without alerting salmon and other fish predators. Phhhhttttt!

You might wonder what we talk about....

BUBBLES ARE FOR POPPING.

Snapping Shrimp • *Alpheus heterochaelis*

Snap! Pop! Pop-pop! Day and night, snapping shrimp in coral reefs slam their snapper claws shut. They do it to communicate, to scare animals away, and to catch prey. But the loud sound is made by a bubble, not the parts of the claw hitting each other. When the snapper claw closes, water squirts out of it. The water moves so fast (about 60 mph, or 100 km/hr) that a bubble forms. The bubble quickly collapses into itself with great force. It's this implosion—like an explosion, but inward—that makes the sound. A colony of shrimp pop-pop-popping away makes quite a racket. In fact, sometimes it's so loud it gets in the way of U.S. Navy sonar.

It's a shrimp thing.

BUBBLES ARE FOR PLAYING.

Bottlenose Dolphin • *Tursiops truncatus*

Young dolphins play with bubbles. They push bubbles around and chase them. It's a game to try and bite the bubbles before they burst at the surface. Some dolphins also make bubble rings. A quick flick of the head starts a small underwater whirlpool. Bubbles enter the whirlpool from the dolphin's blowhole and form a ring about as thick as a pencil and up to two feet wide. Dolphins play with their rings and sometimes bite them, sending thousands of tiny bubbles wiggling to the surface. More rings? No problem. Another flick of the head—and another bubble ring appears.

BUBBLES ARE FOR TASTING—YUCK!

Rattlebox Moth • *Utetheisa ornatrix*

Most moths have drab coloring and fly at night to avoid predators. Not rattlebox moths. They flash their orange stripes and black-and-white polka dots in broad daylight, as if to say, "Nyah, nyah, na-nyah, nyah," to predators. These moths stay alive, though—because they have a secret defense. Their bodies contain a bad-tasting chemical that comes from the plants they eat. When a rattlebox moth is disturbed, a glob of yellow bubbles seeps from either side of its head as a warning. The chemical is so disgusting to spiders that when a rattlebox moth gets caught in a web, the spider will cut the moth loose and let it go.

Shhh . . .

BUBBLES ARE FOR HIDING IN.

Juniper Spittlebug • *Clastoptera juniperina*

Shortly after hatching, juniper spittlebug nymphs begin feeding on the juice from tender juniper stems. The nymphs let out juicy bubbles until their bodies are completely covered in foam. This wet bubble home keeps the nymph from drying out in the hot sun. Not many other insects or animals want to disturb the gooey, bubbly mess, so it makes a great hiding place, too—safe from parasites and predators. Spittlebug nymphs hang around upside down in their "spittle" bubble homes for a month or two until they're ready to molt into adults. Adult spittlebugs fly, walk, and hop from plant to plant. No more bubble homes for them.

Ick!

BUBBLES ARE FOR NESTING.

African Gray Treefrog • *Chiromantis xerampelina*

Most frogs lay eggs in water. The African gray treefrog lays eggs in a nest in a tree! The female frog climbs onto a branch above a pool of water. She releases a thick liquid, and before it has a chance to drip into the pool, she kicks it very fast with her hind legs. Fwap-fwap-fwap-fwap—soon she's whipped the liquid into a big blob of foam. After she lays eggs in this foam nest, male frogs fertilize them, and then the outer bubbles harden. The foam inside stays moist—a perfect place for the eggs to hatch into tadpoles. A few days later, the tadpoles all wiggle out and fall into the water.

BUBBLES ARE FOR
SHOOTING HOOPS.

Pearl Gourami • *Trichogaster leeri*

Fish playing basketball? No, not really. But the way gouramis care for their young sure looks like basketball. The male gourami gulps air from the surface and blows sticky bubbles. A few hundred bubbles together make a floating nest. Then it's time to shoot some hoops. As the female releases eggs, the male swims around and collects them in his mouth. Then he spits each egg into the nest—two points! The male guards the nest until the eggs hatch and the young fish, called fry, are able to swim and feed themselves. Until then, he uses his "basketball" moves to return the eggs and fry that happen to fall out.

38

BUBBLES ARE FOR SAVING ANIMALS.

Human • *Homo sapiens*

Clang! A huge hammer pounds a long steel tube into the bottom of San Francisco Bay. Each tube, called a pile, measures eight feet across and is longer than a football field (330 feet, or 100 meters). The new Bay Bridge will be built on more than one hundred of these piles. Clang! Above the water, it sounds like a giant church bell, but under the water, the sound waves are powerful enough to kill nearby fish. Each pile is pounded thousands of times. That's a lot of dead fish. Construction crews use bubbles to save the fish. They pump air into plastic piping placed around the pile. The air flows through holes in the piping and streams in bubbles to the surface. The curtain of bubbles stops dangerous sound waves from reaching the fish.

More amazing facts about
BUBBLE MAKERS

Snail? What snail?

Violet Sea Snail • *Janthina janthina*
Habitat: Warm ocean surfaces
Where: Worldwide • Size across: 1 inch (3 cm)

Amazing Fact: When sailing on their bubble rafts, violet sea snails are purple on top and almost white on the bottom. This difference in top and bottom color is called countershading. Thanks to countershading, the snails are able to hide out in the open. The darker side blends into the color of the water as seen by birds from the air, while the white side blends into the sunlight as seen by predators from underneath.

So...these pictures aren't to scale?

Water Shrew • *Sorex palustris*
Habitat: Edges of streams and lakes in forested mountain areas
Where: Southern Alaska, west and northeast U.S.,
most of southern Canada • Length: 6 inches (15 cm)

Amazing Facts: As the water shrew dives, a silvery layer of bubbles covers its body, so it must swim hard to reach the bottom. Shrews that stop paddling pop up to the surface like a cork. An adult water shrew weighs about as much as three U.S. nickels, which makes this shrew the smallest of all diving mammals.

Backswimmer • *Notonecta glauca*
Habitat: Ponds, lake edges, small pools, and other still freshwater
Where: Europe • Length: 0.5 inches (1.3 cm)

Amazing Facts: Hairs on the backswimmer's feet, joints, and lower body sense when prey is moving nearby. Backswimmers know which movements are made by something good to eat and which aren't. Backswimmers also have wings, so if a pool or pond dries up, they simply fly to a new one, grab more bubbles from the surface, and dive in.

Maybe they are. Maybe we grew!

Dream on.

Sea Otter • *Enhydra lutris*
Habitat: Ocean
Where: North Pacific • Body length: 40 inches (1 m)

Amazing Facts: Until sea otter pups learn to groom bubbles into their own fur, the mother keeps her pups dry by carrying them on her belly as she floats on her back. Sea otters drift when they're asleep, so sometimes a sea otter will use strands of kelp to anchor itself like a boat. Sea otters have the densest fur of any animal—up to one million hairs per square inch (6.45 square cm).

Water Spider • *Argyroneta aquatica*
Habitat: Still or slow-moving freshwater
Where: Northern and central Europe, Siberia, northern Asia
Length: 0.5 inches (1.3 cm)

Amazing Facts: This is the only spider that spends its whole life underwater. Sitting in its bubble home, it pokes its legs into the water below. When its legs detect prey moving nearby or struggling on the surface, the spider leaves the bubble and pounces. It then brings the prey back to the bubble to eat.

Star-nosed Mole • *Condylura cristata*
Habitat: Wetlands
Where: Eastern Canada, northeastern United States
Body length: 4.5 inches (11 cm)

Amazing Fact: Star-nosed moles breathe bubbles in and out very fast—between five and ten times per second. That's about the same sniffing rate as similar land animals, such as rats and mice.

I smell something BIG.

Humpback Whale • *Megaptera novaeangliae*
Habitat: Ocean
Where: Worldwide, except Arabian Gulf; Mediterranean, Baltic, and Red Seas; and extreme polar regions • Length: 45 feet (14 m)

Amazing Facts: For humpbacks, fishing with bubble nets is almost like a dance. Each whale performs the same moves with each net. One calls, others make the bubble net, and all of the whales leap out of the water in exactly the same order and location, lunge after lunge. You can tell humpback whales apart by looking at their tail markings. No two are the same.

Weddell Seal • *Leptonychotes weddellii*
Habitat: Cold ocean, sea ice
Where: Antarctic • Length: 10 feet (3 m)

Amazing Facts: A Weddell seal can stay underwater for more than an hour at a time, dive ten times deeper than scuba divers can go, and eat hundreds of fish per day. Watching the first seal-cam videos, scientists were surprised to learn that Weddell seals use bubbles to chase fish. These seals also blow bubbles to keep other seals from stealing their breathing holes.

Herring
Clupea pallasii (Pacific); *Clupea harengus* (Atlantic)
Habitat: Ocean, near the coast
Where: (Atlantic herring) North Atlantic, North Sea, Baltic Sea; (Pacific herring) North Pacific • Length: up to 16 inches (40 cm)

Amazing Fact: Herring FaRTs were discovered by accident. When researchers heard the noise coming from a lab down the hall, they thought the fish scientists were being rude. The fish scientists thought the researchers were playing a joke on them—until they realized the sounds were coming from a herring tank in which someone had left the microphone turned on.

Snapping Shrimp • *Alpheus heterochaelis*
Habitat: Shallow tropical and subtropical ocean waters, coral reefs
Where: Worldwide • Length: 2 inches (5 cm)

Amazing Facts: These pinkie-sized shrimp have one claw that is much larger than the other. This claw makes bubbles. Each collapsing bubble makes a short, bright flash of light and bit of extreme heat—up to 36,000° F (20,000° C). That's hotter than the surface of the sun! Next time you're snorkeling and you hear the sound of popcorn popping, look for a colony of snapping shrimp.

Bottlenose Dolphin • *Tursiops truncatus*
Habitat: Ocean • Where: Worldwide, except in polar regions
Length: 6 to 13 feet (2 to 4 m)

Amazing Facts: Dolphins learn from other dolphins how to make bubble rings. It takes practice to get it right. Some dolphins can send bubble rings traveling in different directions, make one bubble ring by joining two rings together, or make a ring larger by adding more air. Scientists haven't found a practical reason for the bubble rings. Dolphins appear to make them just for fun.

Tasty, tasty fish . . .

Swim for it!

Better make it snappy!

Flashy works for me.

Rattlebox Moth • *Utetheisa ornatrix*
Habitat: Forest edges, fields
Where: North America (east of Arizona, south of Ontario) to northern South America, Bermuda, Bahamas, Greater Antilles
Wingspan: 1.5 inches (4 cm)

Amazing Facts: The yucky-tasting chemical made by the rattlebox moth is called pyrrolizidine alkaloid, or PA, for short. It protects the eggs from ants and ladybugs, as well as protecting the larvae and adult moths from spiders. Female rattlebox moths prefer mates that have a large amount of PA.

Western Spittlebug • *Clastoptera juniperina*
Habitat: Juniper trees and shrubs
Where: North America (Rocky Mountains and west)
Length: 0.34 inches (1 cm)

Amazing Facts: It takes 15 to 30 minutes for a spittlebug to make enough bubbles to completely cover its body. Spittlebugs don't usually cause serious problems for the plants they feed on, but sometimes many spittlebugs share the same plant, which can cause damage.

Peek-a-boo!

Happy landings!

African Gray Treefrog • *Chiromantis xerampelina*
Habitat: Savanna
Where: Southeastern tip of Africa • Length: 3 inches (7 cm)

Amazing Facts: A foam nest contains around 850 eggs, each about the size of the head of a pin. The foam contains oxygen eggs need. The tadpoles drop from the nest all at once. Nests are made at night and may take several hours to complete.

Pearl Gourami • *Trichogaster leeri*
Habitat: Rivers with many plants, often stagnant water
Where: Thailand, Malaysia, Indonesia • Length: 4 inches (10 cm)

Amazing Fact: Unlike most fish, which get oxygen from the water around them, gouramis get oxygen from air breathed at the surface. So gouramis are able to live in stagnant water with little oxygen, where other fish can't survive. Bubble nests keep the gourami eggs near the surface, where oxygen is plentiful.

Human • *Homo sapiens*
Habitat: All kinds • Where: Worldwide

Amazing Fact: Ships go into drydock, a special docking pen, when they need to be out of water for repairs. A bubble curtain at the entrance lets ships enter, but keeps animals safely outside. Before bubble curtains, fish and seals would swim into drydock with the ships, and then get stuck once the water drained. Bubbles to the rescue!

Dry docks are NOT fish-friendly.

This mom never says, "No spitting!"

GLOSSARY • INDEX

Baleen plates: Baleen is made of fingernail-like material called keratin. Baleen plates are strips of baleen that hang like a curtain inside the mouth of the humpback whale. Baleen plates let water through, but catch fish and other sea animals inside the whale's mouth. A quick lick and a gulp, and then it's on to the next mouthful of water to continue the meal. Other filter-feeding whales have baleen, too. *p. 20*

Blowhole: The hole on top of a whale or dolphin's head. Whales and dolphins breathe through their blowholes. *p. 29*

FaRTs: Short for "Fast Repetitive Ticks," the name scientists made up for the farting noise herring make. It sounds like farting, but it isn't real farting, because the gas that makes the sound comes from air the herring gulp at the surface. In true farting (flatulence), gas comes from the food an animal eats. *p. 24*

Fertilize: When a male's sperm combines with a female's eggs so that the eggs may develop into young. *p. 34*

Flatulence: The scientific name for farting. *p. 24*

Fry: Baby fish. *p. 36*

Hibernate: To spend the winter in a deep, sleeplike state. *p. 16*

Larva: A young insect that isn't fully grown into an adult yet. Larvae (more than one larva) look very different from their parents. A caterpillar is an example of a larva. *p. 13*

Molt: To shed skin, fur, or feathers. Some animals molt in the fall to grow warmer fur for winter. Insects molt to grow larger. *p. 33*

Nymph: A young insect that isn't fully grown into an adult yet. It looks like its parents, but must molt again before being able to fly and make young. *pp. 10, 33*

Parasite: An animal that lives in or on another animal, called the host. Parasites feed on their hosts or on the food their hosts have eaten. *p. 33*

Piles: Strong metal, wood, or concrete posts pounded into the ground on which people build docks, bridges, or buildings. *p. 39*

Predator: An animal that hunts or kills other animals. *pp. 24, 33*

Prey: An animal hunted or killed for food by other animals. *pp. 13, 16, 27*

Scientists have a fancy word for everything!

They sure do.

Cool!

44

ACKNOWLEDGMENTS

I wish to thank the following scientists and scholars around the globe who answered all my questions; generously shared their research, labs, expertise, and experiences, as well as a few laughs and some critter-cam footage; and reviewed the manuscript:

Dr. Lance Barrett-Lennard and Jen Reynolds, Vancouver Aquarium Marine Science Centre; Dr. Jim Bodkin, Alaska Science Center, USGS; Dr. Gary Caldwell, Newcastle University, Newcastle upon Tyne, UK; Dr. Randall Davis, Texas A&M University at Galveston; Dr. Larry Dill, Simon Fraser University, and the Alaska-British Columbia Whale Foundation; Dr. Thomas Eisner, Cornell University; Dr. Andy Hamilton, Canadian National Collection of Insects, Arachnids and Nematodes; Chris Himes, the Burke Museum of Natural History and Culture, WA; Dr. Elaine Humphrey, University of British Columbia BioImaging Facility; Dr. Michael Jennions, the Australian National University; Andy Johnson, Monterey Bay Aquarium; Dr. Nancy Knowlton, Scripps Institution of Oceanography of the University of California, San Diego, and Smithsonian Tropical Research Institute; Dr. John F. Pagels, Virginia Commonwealth University; James Reyff, Illingworth & Rodkin, Inc., Acoustical Engineering; Dr. Paul Seldon, the Natural History Museum, London, UK; Dr. Michel Versluis, University of Twente, The Netherlands; Dr. Reese Voshell, Virginia Tech; Don White, Project Delphis; Dr. Terrie Williams, University of California, Santa Cruz.

Thank you to Carolyn for finding the perfect way to express the science, whimsy, and heart of my words; a bow to Roxyanne Young and Kelly Milner Halls, without whom this book could still be sitting in my Ideas File; and my thanks and love to Michael, Teri, Jonathan, and Dessa, the folks who share my bubble.